"Officers should be most punctilious in their dealings with servants as with all other soldiers. Undue familiarity tends to break up the whole scheme of discipline and lowers the standards of respect for Officers as a class."
HINTS FOR YOUNG OFFICERS, MAJOR H.T. COCK, M.C. (1931)

"Wherever you go and whatever you are doing, as long as you have a partner for the occasion, your first duty is to see to it that your partner has all the attention you can offer."
VENTURE TRAINING MANUAL NO. 1, NEPTUNE'S NOTES, "NEPTUNUS REX," ROYAL CANADIAN NAVY (CIRCA 1950s)

"If you are sentinel at the tent of one of the Field-Officers, you need not challenge in the fore part of the evening, for fear of disturbing his honor, who perhaps may be reading, writing, or entertaining company. But as soon as he is gone to bed, roar out every ten minutes at least, 'Who comes there?' though nobody is passing. This will give him a favorable idea of your alertness; and though his slumbers may be broken, yet will they be the more pleasing, when he finds that he reposes in perfect security. When the hour of relief approaches, keep constantly crying out, 'Relief, relief!' It will prevent the guard from forgetting you, and prove that you are not asleep."
ADVICE TO THE OFFICERS OF THE BRITISH ARMY, ANON. (1872)

"However tempted you may be, do not dwell too much on your own doings; however interesting they may be to you, others are not likely to be equally interested and will look upon you as that pest of all bachelor gatherings, the 'Club bore.'"
CUSTOMS OF THE SERVICE (ADVICE TO THOSE NEWLY COMMISSIONED), A.H.S. (1939)

"You should cultivate a personal knowledge of all of the enlisted men whom you command, or with whom you come in frequent contact; however, you should scrupulously avoid such intimacy as may tend to result in a loss of respect, or breed familiarity on their part. Your social activities should be separate from enlisted men."
HINTS FOR NEWLY COMMISSIONED OFFICERS, MAJOR GENERAL J. A. ULIO (FEBRUARY, 1943)

*"You are sure to get some queer-looking fellows to command at times.
They may, at first sight—and at second sight, too—seem fairly hopeless material."*
COMRADES IN ARMS: THREE TALKS TO JUNIOR OFFICERS OR OFFICER CADETS TO ASSIST THEM
IN THE HANDLING OF THEIR MEN, THE CHIEF OF THE IMPERIAL GENERAL STAFF (JUNE, 1942)

"Don't try to 'take over' the club. I have seen this done by enthusiastic Cadets gathering in a group around the bar and getting slightly tipsy to the point where they have started to raise their voices in song. This disturbs the other guests, so if you feel the temptation, even if you are encouraged by one of the members of the club (there will always be one who doesn't give a damn) I advise you not to."

VENTURE TRAINING MANUAL NO. 1, NEPTUNE'S NOTES, "NEPTUNUS REX," ROYAL CANADIAN NAVY (CIRCA 1950s)

"Whenever you mount guard, invite all your friends to the guardroom; and not only get drunk yourself, but make your company drunk also; and then sing and make as much noise as possible. This will show the world the difference between an Officer and a private man; since the latter would be flayed alive for the least irregularity upon duty."
ADVICE TO THE OFFICERS OF THE BRITISH ARMY, ANON. (1872)

" . . . Let your deportment be haughty and insolent to your inferiors,
humble and fawning to your superiors, solemn and distant to your equals . . . "
ADVICE TO THE OFFICERS OF THE BRITISH ARMY, ANON. (1872)

"There is nothing which benefits a man more, or is more enjoyable, than the right kind of drink in the right place at the right time. Choose your drink with at least the same care that you would your food. Unless you wish to appear uneducated in these matters, never drink more than one sherry or other short drink before a meal; you will spoil your palate."
CUSTOMS OF THE SERVICE (ADVICE TO THOSE NEWLY COMMISSIONED), A.H.S. (1939)

*"Do things with your men. Not just the nice things like playing games with them,
though that is very important, but the unpleasant ones, too . . . It's worth it every time."*
COMRADES IN ARMS: THREE TALKS TO JUNIOR OFFICERS OR OFFICER CADETS TO ASSIST THEM
IN THE HANDLING OF THEIR MEN, THE CHIEF OF THE IMPERIAL GENERAL STAFF (JUNE, 1942)

"... Treat Mrs. Colonel as if she were the embodiment of the Mona Lisa, Cleopatra, and your mother. Enquire after her health, dance with her eldest spotty daughter, and after dinner at the house use expressions like, 'Golly gosh, just like my mother's cooking!' Deprecate the philandering of your friends with a wistful little smile that speaks volumes for your self-control and your worldliness. Try to be nice to the spotty daughter (she may just grow into a swan)."
HOW TO BE A SUCCESSFUL SUBALTERN, "SUSTAINER" (1978)

"If your General keeps a girl, it is your duty to squire her to all public places ..."
ADVICE TO THE OFFICERS OF THE BRITISH ARMY, ANON. (1872)

"Always ask for leave at all times and in all places. In the end, you will acquire a kind of right to it."
THE YOUNG OFFICER'S GUIDE TO KNOWLEDGE, "THE SENIOR MAJOR" (1915)

"Port, etc. is served at the conclusion of dinner, followed by coffee, followed in turn by cigars and cigarettes. Officers should avail themselves of the cigars and cigarettes handed around before producing their own smoking materials. Pipe smoking at table is absolutely taboo. Smoking will not commence until after the toast has been honored, nor until the Senior Officer present commences or has given permission to smoke."
HINTS FOR YOUNG OFFICERS, MAJOR H.T. COCK, M.C. (1931)

"Ever since the days of Ancient Pistol, we find that a large and broad-rimmed beaver has been peculiar to heroes. A hat of this kind worn over your right eye, with two large dangling tassels, and a proportionate cockade and feather, will give you an air of courage and martial gallantry."
ADVICE TO THE OFFICERS OF THE BRITISH ARMY, ANON. (1872)

"By his conduct in his own and other Service Messes, an Officer can bring credit, but much more quickly discredit, to himself and the Service to which he has the honor to belong. Informality in a Mess may be carried too far on occasions. Nothing is more deplorable than to hear a Junior Officer addressing his Commanding Officer as 'Old Boy.'"
CUSTOMS OF THE SERVICE (ADVICE TO THOSE NEWLY COMMISSIONED), A.H.S. (1939)

"In loading the baggage you have an opportunity of obliging the ladies of the regiment: but remember never to let an ugly woman ride in a convenient or elevated station, as she might disgrace the corps."
ADVICE TO THE OFFICERS OF THE BRITISH ARMY, ANON. (1872)

"Remember your primary duty as a guest is to help keep things going. DON'T head for the best-looking girl in the party, unless she happens to be standing by herself. DO go straight to any female woman of the opposite sex who happens to be temporarily unoccupied and start talking to her. It matters not one bit whether she is half or twice your age—what does matter is that she is another guest for whom your Hostess is responsible and it is up to you as another guest to help her enjoy the party also."
VENTURE TRAINING MANUAL NO. 1, NEPTUNE'S NOTES, "NEPTUNUS REX," ROYAL CANADIAN NAVY (CIRCA 1950s)

"When you escort a man to the field for punishment, you may let him drink as much liquor as he can procure.
This will, in some measure, deaden the pain, and prevent him from disgracing himself and the regiment,
by becoming what the drummers term 'a nightingale.'"
ADVICE TO THE OFFICERS OF THE BRITISH ARMY, ANON. (1872)

"The Army does not officially recognise the marriage of an officer until he is 25 years of age. The reason for this is that a young officer has much to learn before he becomes fully proficient . . . Man management is best learnt by being with the men as much as possible, both on parade and off parade, playing games, or organising their sports and recreation. If an officer marries young he is bound to have extra interests outside his Army life and his work and learning will suffer."
CUSTOMS OF THE ARMY, THE CHIEF OF THE IMPERIAL GENERAL STAFF, THE WAR OFFICE (1956)

"*If it is the custom of your regiment for the soldiers to be cured of the venereal disease gratis, give yourself but little concern about them, and be sure to treat them as roughly as possible. Tenderness towards patients of that kind is only an encouragement of vice; and if you make a perfect and speedy cure, they will soon forget the inconveniences of the disorder; where as they carry some mementos about them, it will make them thence-forward the more cautious.*"
ADVICE TO THE OFFICERS OF THE BRITISH ARMY, ANON. (1872)

"Don't handle the man; make him correct minor faults himself,
or you can check serious faults for disciplinary action."
HINTS FOR YOUNG OFFICERS, MAJOR H.T. COCK, M.C. (1931)

*"On no account inquire into the private domestic affairs of your married men;
leave that until you are in command. You are too young at present and they would resent it."*
HINTS FOR NEWLY COMMISSIONED OFFICERS, MAJOR GENERAL J. A. ULIO (FEBRUARY, 1943)

"There is no objection whatsoever to having any male visitor into your cabin but naturally this does not apply to visitors of the gentler sex."
VENTURE TRAINING MANUAL NO. 1, NEPTUNE'S NOTES, "NEPTUNUS REX," ROYAL CANADIAN NAVY (CIRCA 1950s)

"If there should be a soberly-disposed person, or, in other words, a fellow of no spirit, in the corps, you must not only bore him constantly at the Mess, but should make use of a kind of practical wit to torment him. Thus you may force open his doors, break his windows, damage his furniture, and put wh—s in his bed; or in camp throw squibs and crackers into his tent at night, or loosen his tent-cords in windy weather. Young gentlemen will never be at a loss for contrivances of this nature."
ADVICE TO THE OFFICERS OF THE BRITISH ARMY, ANON. (1872)

"Should an officer be late for dinner, he should apologize to the President, at the head of the table, before taking his seat."
HINTS FOR YOUNG OFFICERS, MAJOR H.T. COCK, M.C. (1931)

"You cannot take too much pains to maintain subordination in your corps. The subalterns of the British army are but too apt to think themselves gentlemen; a mistake which it is your business to rectify. Put them, as often as you can; upon the most disagreeable and ungentlemanly duties; and endeavor by every means to bring them upon a level with the subaltern Officers of the German armies."

ADVICE TO THE OFFICERS OF THE BRITISH ARMY, ANON. (1872)

"Be friendly with the men without being familiar. That is a lot easier to say than to do, and I think that this is one of the hardest problems that a young Officer has to solve: Just how far can he go with his men?"

COMRADES IN ARMS: THREE TALKS TO JUNIOR OFFICERS OR OFFICER CADETS TO ASSIST THEM IN THE HANDLING OF THEIR MEN, THE CHIEF OF THE IMPERIAL GENERAL STAFF (JUNE, 1942)

"Be sure to listen to every piece of scandal respecting the Commanding Officer, and tell him of it the first opportunity. Should none be thrown out, it might not be amiss to invent some. If he keeps a lady, wait upon her with the utmost respect, be her chaperone to all public places, feed her dog, and scratch the poll of her parrot—but take care that your attention to the lady does not make her keeper jealous."
ADVICE TO THE OFFICERS OF THE BRITISH ARMY, ANON. (1872)

"Officers should be exact in their turnout either in uniform or mufti at all times. An Officer will always change for dinner. If permitted to dine in mufti, he will wear evening dress. Changing for supper is a matter for the custom of the unit concerned."
HINTS FOR YOUNG OFFICERS, MAJOR H.T. COCK, M.C. (1931)

"Your responsibilities do not end with working hours; it is equally important to take a genuine interest in their activities after the day's work is done. While you are young and single is the easiest time to do this... Make the most of your opportunities now... When the men find you really do take an interest, their whole-hearted co-operation, not only in their leisure-hour activities, but on duty as well, will more than repay you."
HINTS FOR NEWLY COMMISSIONED OFFICERS, MAJOR GENERAL J. A. ULIO (FEBRUARY, 1943)

"... Remember that merely offering negative sex advice, with the emphasis on the evils of promiscuity, will cut very little ice with most young men, and will very likely do more harm than good."
COMRADES IN ARMS: THREE TALKS TO JUNIOR OFFICERS OR OFFICER CADETS TO ASSIST THEM IN THE HANDLING OF THEIR MEN, THE CHIEF OF THE IMPERIAL GENERAL STAFF (JUNE, 1942)

"Confine the soldiers as often as possible. This will afford you an opportunity of obliging them, or their wives, by getting them off again . . . "

ADVICE TO THE OFFICERS OF THE BRITISH ARMY, ANON. (1872)

*"Good drill undoubtedly raises the morale of all ranks; the pride in doing something well;
precision and smartness still appeals to most."*
HINTS FOR YOUNG OFFICERS, MAJOR H.T. COCK, M.C. (1931)

"A man who has travelled extensively or had the advantages of unusual experiences is interesting and sometimes amusing, as long as he does not overdo it."
CUSTOMS OF THE SERVICE (ADVICE TO THOSE NEWLY COMMISSIONED), A.H.S. (1939)

"In uniform, Officers, when not wearing a sword, carry a straight swagger cane without a crook or handle. It must not exceed 23" in length."
HINTS FOR YOUNG OFFICERS, MAJOR H.T. COCK, M.C. (1931)

"So far as is humanly possible, keep men who are pals together. As you know, having a good half section, or a good mate, means a great deal to a soldier . . . Separating pals unnecessarily is one of those unnecessary hardships which men quite rightly resent and grouse about . . . "
COMRADES IN ARMS: THREE TALKS TO JUNIOR OFFICERS OR OFFICER CADETS TO ASSIST THEM
IN THE HANDLING OF THEIR MEN, THE CHIEF OF THE IMPERIAL GENERAL STAFF (JUNE, 1942)

"... Troops will stand fast on line reached at that hour which will be reported to Brigade Hdqrs ...
There will be no intercourse of any description with the enemy ... Further instructions follow."
MESSAGES AND SIGNALS, CAPTAIN MICHAEL O'LEARY (NOVEMBER, 1918)

"On the rear guard, when the Sergeant has left you (which he will infallibly do, soon after he has mounted) you become the Commanding Officer, and have an opportunity of obliging the soldiers."
ADVICE TO THE OFFICERS OF THE BRITISH ARMY, ANON. (1872)

"Never listen to or indulge in loose gossip concerning women in the Mess. Traditional chivalry of Officers through the ages has forbidden this . . . it is up to you to keep this excellent custom, and do not let it be said that Officers of today are less chivalrous than those of the past."
CUSTOMS OF THE SERVICE (ADVICE TO THOSE NEWLY COMMISSIONED), A.H.S. (1939)

"Evening roll-calling, which drags one from the bottle, is a most unmilitary custom: for drinking is as essential a part of an Officer's duty as fighting."
ADVICE TO THE OFFICERS OF THE BRITISH ARMY, ANON. (1872)

"Don't get too close to a man; stand off about three paces so you can really see him."
HINTS FOR YOUNG OFFICERS, MAJOR H.T. COCK, M.C. (1931)

" . . . You who are young, intelligent, and active must have some outlet for these mental and physical energies or if you don't you are going to wind up either introverted or in trouble."
VENTURE TRAINING MANUAL NO. 1, NEPTUNE'S NOTES, "NEPTUNUS REX," ROYAL CANADIAN NAVY (CIRCA 1950s)

"During dinner, however, it is not acceptable to throw food, sugar, or generally carry on in a brash, loud manner. Before you throw the Commanding Officer out the dining room window or roll the Adjutant down the hill outside the Mess, ensure that he will receive the gesture in the same spirit as it is offered."
IN AID OF FEWER EXTRAS AND AN EASIER LIFE IN THE SUBALTERNS' MESS,
THE ROYAL CANADIAN REGIMENT (1977)

"Never remain in a public bar if other ranks are present. It is unfair to them, particularly if you are recognized as an officer, as it cramps their style, and it is unsuitable for you to do so."
HINTS FOR NEWLY COMMISSIONED OFFICERS, MAJOR GENERAL J. A. ULIO (FEBRUARY, 1943)

"All Officers are expected to take a keen interest in the recreation of the Non-Commissioned Officers and men and by their encouragement and example to stimulate every form of sport."
STANDING ORDERS OF THE ROYAL CANADIAN REGIMENT (1935)

"Never reprove or talk to a drunken man; telephone the nearest Service police if possible. The man himself may not be in a condition to understand you and aggravate his offence by using insulting language, or even worse."
HINTS FOR NEWLY COMMISSIONED OFFICERS, MAJOR GENERAL J. A. ULIO (FEBRUARY, 1943)

"For an Officer to write a cheque or a demand on a field cashier for more than he has in the bank, without prior arrangement with the bank, is not only dishonest but also disgraceful. A dishonored cheque may lead to a Court Martial."
CUSTOMS OF THE ARMY, THE CHIEF OF THE IMPERIAL GENERAL STAFF, THE WAR OFFICE (1956)

"... On personal cleanliness: I honestly do not believe, from my experience of him, that the New Army young Officer omits to wash; quite contrariwise. But he does, at times, cut a queer figure in uniform!"
AN OPEN LETTER TO THE VERY YOUNG OFFICER, C. N. W. (NOVEMBER, 1917)

"When the table is cleared prior to the service of port, the servants are expected to remove all other glasses, etc., whether empty or not. Officers should be careful not to interfere with this arrangement."
HINTS FOR YOUNG OFFICERS, MAJOR H.T. COCK, M.C. (1931)

"Many enlisted men will imitate the Officers who command them. It is therefore essential that you set the highest example. This applies not only to your performance of routine duties but to your personal appearance and habits."
HINTS FOR NEWLY COMMISSIONED OFFICERS, MAJOR GENERAL J. A. ULIO (FEBRUARY, 1943)

"Ladies expect to have doors opened for them, to have their cigarettes lit and ashtrays provided for them—Bless them! Help them on and off with their coats and be prepared to do anything for them, except lend them money."

VENTURE TRAINING MANUAL NO. 1, NEPTUNE'S NOTES, "NEPTUNUS REX," ROYAL CANADIAN NAVY (CIRCA 1950s)

"An Officer must obtain his Commanding Officer's permission before getting married."
CUSTOMS OF THE ARMY, THE CHIEF OF THE IMPERIAL GENERAL STAFF, THE WAR OFFICE (1956)

"Dinner, however, is a parade. Punctuality is essential and every Officer should make a point of being in the ante-room at least five minutes before the dinner hour. No smoking is permitted in the ante-room before dinner, nor for half an hour previous to dinner."
HINTS FOR YOUNG OFFICERS, MAJOR H.T. COCK, M.C. (1931)

*"Avoid debts. Budget your salary and live within it. If you must gamble,
do so with Officers of approximately the same income as your own."*
HINTS FOR NEWLY COMMISSIONED OFFICERS, MAJOR GENERAL J. A. ULIO (FEBRUARY, 1943)

"When your General invites any subalterns to his table, it will be unbecoming your dignity to take any notice of them. If there are any Field Officers or Captains invited, you may condescend to chatter and hob-nob with them."
ADVICE TO THE OFFICERS OF THE BRITISH ARMY, ANON. (1872)

"Never curse Mess servants; it is not clever and they cannot stand up for themselves without danger of dismissal. Make any complaint you have to the Mess Secretary, who will take proper steps to deal with it."
HINTS FOR NEWLY COMMISSIONED OFFICERS, MAJOR GENERAL J. A. ULIO (FEBRUARY, 1943)

"It is customary for Officers to carry a stick when walking in mufti."
HINTS FOR YOUNG OFFICERS, MAJOR H.T. COCK, M.C. (1931)

"Profanity has no place in the vocabulary of an Officer."
HINTS FOR NEWLY COMMISSIONED OFFICERS, MAJOR GENERAL J. A. ULIO (FEBRUARY, 1943)